PARISIAN INTERIORS

This book is dedicated to the memory
of Madeleine Castaing

PARISIAN INTERIORS

BOLD · ELEGANT · REFINED

BARBARA & RENÉ STOELTIE
Foreword by JACQUES GARCIA

Flammarion

Acknowledgments

We never would have been able to complete this work without the gracious collaboration of all those who opened the doors of their *hôtel particulier*, apartment, loft, or "dacha in the attic" to us. We also would like to thank Mr. Lenny Kravitz and our friends M. Jacques Garcia and M. Yves Gastou and, last but not least, Mme Hélène David-Weill and Mme Sylvie Legrand-Rossi, who gave us access to one of the finest jewels of French decorative art, the Musée Nissim de Camondo. Thanks to them, what could have been a grueling task was transformed into a fascinating adventure.

Text and photo styling
Barbara Stoeltie

Photographs and layout
René Stoeltie

Technical assistance
Limelight Laboratory

Translated from the French by
Nicole Alves

Copyediting
Lise Connellan

Typesetting
Juliette de Patoul

Coordination
Geneviève Defrance

Color separation
Graphart

Printed in Italy by
Graphart

Originally published in French as *La Magie de Paris*

www.fondsmercator.be

Exclusive distribution of the English-language edition

Flammarion, s.a.
87, quai Panhard et Levassor
75647 Paris Cedex 13
www.editions.flammarion.com

11 12 13 3 2 1

ISBN 978-2-08-030172-7
Dépôt légal: 01/2011

CONTENTS

FOREWORD

Paris is a city of contrasts. Contrasts conferred on it by the mixed character of its population and by the unceasing hospitality it offers to those who have a taste for radical change.

The French are not a subdued people, and Paris follows this example by translating the need for excitement and new forms through its constantly changing appearance. You do not build a new temple over the ruins of the old, and in Paris this golden rule has been followed for centuries in an acute fever of demolition and construction—a collective frenzy that has seen countless buildings and even whole neighborhoods disappear, only to be reconstructed. For example, in the nineteenth century, Baron Haussmann demolished beautiful mansions and eighteenth-century follies to erect his own extravagances in their place: the Grands Boulevards. A century later, the "belly of Paris"—the vast central market—was razed and the gaping hole was filled with a blatantly futuristic Les Halles and the nearby "Beaubourg." And more recently, the construction of La Défense and its Grande Arche, and the Bastille Opera have left an unforgettable visual imprint on the city.

Paris loves the transformation process and in no way opposes the iconoclastic spirit of its innovators and constant critics. The city's architecture and interior decoration have experienced more styles and trends in the last two centuries than in the rest of the two millennia of Christian civilization put together. And *mea culpa, mea maxima culpa*, I willingly confess to having often contributed to these changing interiors and having created controversy in this fundamental field; persisting to the point of utter stubbornness, and going against the tide.

Paris is no white and beige city. Paris is bubbly, cheerful, crazy, grand, elegant, exuberant, provocative, haunting, and vulgar—it is shameless. The interiors portrayed on these pages demonstrate this personality, and the individuals who created them provide undeniable proof that creativity and boldness make for a good partnership.

"Everything is created in Paris, everything comes to Paris, and everything comes from Paris!" declared the late Madeleine Castaing when the avant-garde spirit of London or New York was praised. And, as usual, Madeleine had the last word.

— Jacques Garcia

INTRODUCTION

During her honeymoon in Paris, in 1954, my aunt bought me two gifts: a dreadfully ugly plastic pen—complete with a magnifying lens displaying the Eiffel Tower—and an equally awful snowdome containing a plastic model of the Sacré-Cœur with a wretched little pile of snow that allowed me to create my own blizzard around the famous basilica. However, these souvenirs intended for tasteless tourists did not prevent me from truly falling in love with the French capital, whose culture and beauty—and especially the combination of both—from that moment forward instilled in me an unshakable faith before becoming—although only briefly—my home base. *Paris is always Paris.* For me, too. Paris and its stunning monuments, elegant boulevards, the kitschy charm of the place du Tertre, and the past glory of Montparnasse, or the artistic atmosphere of Belleville. The Paris of Mistinguett, Chevalier, and Piaf. An accordion and a glass of ruby red wine sipped during a moment of reflection on a terrace. However, beyond the Paris of overused clichés, an unsuspected task awaited me: to describe what hides behind the beautiful facades of its buildings.

Anyone who has lived in Paris has experienced the exhilaration of these discoveries. Long walks through the city, exploring every little corner and, above all, taking a peek behind the facades. For René and me this was a true quest to find the most distinctive, captivating, surprising, intriguing, dazzling, and spiritual interior spaces, generated by the imaginations of the most diverse personalities: artists, designers, architects, businessmen, collectors, notable residents, and the inevitable eccentric. The world is made up of a little bit of everything ... wealth and poverty, inventiveness and conservatism, classicism and the avant-garde, ingenuity and innovation. For interior design spies brimming with curiosity like René and myself, Paris has unexpected splendors. Armed with a camera and a pen, we easily accessed the most fascinating interiors and few doors remained closed to us. Thus, this book was born. A book about a city of incontrovertible magic. In short, a book about the magic of Paris.

A SUMPTUOUS ESTATE

Lenny Kravitz

A SUMPTUOUS ESTATE

Magnetic Paris has attracted artists from around the world for generations. Painters, writers, musicians, singers, composers, sculptors, architects, furniture makers, designers … the list of creative individuals is so long and so impressive that it could fill the pages of this book. Unable to resist Paris's charms, the celebrated American musician, songwriter, and producer Lenny Kravitz decided to create a base in the capital.

Described by the press and by fans as a key representative of the pop, rock, soul, folk, and funk movements, this musician—the son of a Russian television producer and an actress originally from the Bahamas—who plays a multitude of instruments (guitar, keyboard, drums, bass, and percussion), also has a passion for contemporary art and interior design. His interest is so great that he created his own interior design firm, Kravitz Design, Inc. (KDI) in 2003. Three years later, KDI demonstrated its remarkable talent for interior design in decorating Kravitz's new town house in Paris, built in 1928 to an eighteenth-century model.

Kravitz's house has the majestic glamour and generous proportions characteristic of Parisian town houses. Sensitive to this degree of elegance, Kravitz accented the spectacular entrance hall and sweeping staircase without being overcome by the extravagance of the spaces or the suite of oak-paneled reception rooms or the living room and rotunda bedroom whose high windows overlook a lush garden. Instinctively, Kravitz and his team at KDI understood "how far was too far" and set limits, even though they were working with unlimited resources. The result is a design that is distinguished by a simple elegance despite the spectacular collection of art and furniture. This includes a Schimmel grand piano finished in Plexiglas; artwork by Jean-Michel Basquiat, Emile Gilioli, and Andy Warhol; a vast collection of black-and-white photographs of musician colleagues and family members; numerous Baccarat crystal chandeliers; and a Swarovski crystal chandelier by KDI; vintage lights; and furniture by Joe Colombo, Achille Castiglioni, Paul Evans, Karl Springer, Pedro Friedeberg, Gabriella Crespi, and Bartholo Pucci, most of which was sourced by KDI in New York and Paris.

Kravitz, expressing his passion for interior design, draws inspiration from the past while remaining thoroughly contemporary. His nostalgia for an ancestral and distant land is reflected in his oversized polished steel bed, the bathroom of Calcutta marble featuring a spacious shower, his selection of super soft rugs, and his preference for a warm color palette. Further proof of his nostalgic sensibilities is evident in his impressive collection of stage costumes that once belonged to Jimi Hendrix, Bob Marley, John Lennon, Miles Davis, and James Brown. You can truly sense that this exceptional artist, who continues to get top billing, found a means to express what touches the depths of his being through the interior design of his Paris house.

A BUCOLIC OASIS IN THE HEART OF PARIS

Jean-Luc Gaüzère

A BUCOLIC OASIS IN THE HEART OF PARIS

Paris is full of prestigious, enchanting addresses, and rue de Lille is undeniably one of them. Jean-Luc Gaüzère, a Paris lawyer, moved here a quarter-century ago, into the first floor of a beautiful town house close to the Musée d'Orsay. At that time he would never have suspected that he would leave this place, only to return many years later.

Some houses remain etched in the memory of those who have left them, becoming part of their destiny. Having "traveled" within Paris, around France's countryside, then Italy and Greece, Jean-Luc moved back to the rue de Lille to be reunited with the sumptuous interior that he had never forgotten.

Going back to a place where one has lived can be disappointing because one may seek the familiar decor and atmosphere only to find that they no longer exist. Gaüzère was pleasantly surprised to find the apartment he had once opulently furnished almost completely intact. He discovered that those who had followed him had not touched the beautiful entrance hall with its staircase of Burgundy stone with a gorgeous wrought iron railing, or the central rotunda lined with trompe l'oeil paneling painted by students of Brussels's acclaimed Van der Kelen School of Decorative Arts. The classical architecture of the dining room and living room, whose windows open onto a courtyard where you can hear birds singing, also remained untouched.

In this bucolic oasis in the heart of Paris, behind ruffled silk curtains, Jean-Luc reconstructed from memory what he thought had been lost: the interior style cultivated by an avid collector and traveler who has amassed treasures from all around the world. Here, happiness is found with a hammered silver throne from an Indian palace and portraits of maharajas draped in luxurious jewels, artifacts, and memorabilia worthy of a Russian aristocrat, Empire and eighteenth-century furniture, a white marble scaled-down version of *The Egyptian* who appears in the rue de Sèvres fountain, and sofas, armchairs, and folding chairs covered with richly colored velvets and silks. All these objects are tangible evidence of the exquisite taste and discerning eye of the host.

On rue de Lille, at home with Gaüzère, within a building whose facade has been stripped of ornament, nostalgia reigns. Nostalgia for a place and a home that Gaüzère thought he had lost forever and has resurrected with the greatest skill and sensitivity.

A MERCURIAL TALENT

Roberto Bergero

A MERCURIAL TALENT

The Argentine designer Roberto Bergero deserves a mention in the *Guinness Books of World Records* because no other designer has moved house as often as he has.

Roberto does not seem at all tired by his many travels and the endless to-ings and fro-ings between his apartment in Buenos Aires and his pied-à-terre in Paris, not to mention his frequent moves within the Argentine capital. Compiling a complete list of his relocations is impossible because, in our case, we have viewed only a portion of the properties in which he has lived: a studio on the Butte Montmartre, an entresol in Barbès, an apartment on rue Marcadet, a water mill in the Nivernais region, and his latest dwelling, that occupies one floor in a building close to the Bastille. What is most surprising is that Roberto changes the decor of his lodgings to his liking and at an alarming rate. It is not uncommon to visit his home one evening for dinner, and then discover that everything has changed the next day when you drop in for coffee!

Bergero is a man of great talent. He "can do anything with his hands," and does not hesitate to climb a ladder to decorate his parlor with Velázquez-inspired frescoes, to paint his living room Versailles Gray or Shocking Pink, or to make plaster chandeliers, gilded stucco appliqués, ever-changing taffeta curtains, a miniature four-poster bed for his dog, hand-painted canvas rugs, and anything else that may enhance beauty and the *art de vivre*. His clients obediently follow his lead and—almost always—accept his crazy ideas, no longer surprised that their designer may show them a Montmartre apartment bursting with baroque objects and furniture one week, and then a Directoire setting, furnished with Gustavian sofas and daybeds the following week. Bergero is Bergero, and although he decorated what he declared was the "last" stage of his Parisian oeuvre in "pearl gray, like an eighteenth-century marquis in a white wig," it wasn't long before the gray was replaced with Tyrrhenian Pink, to which Apple Green plaster medallions, neoclassical busts, and bird-nest–shaped appliqués were added.

The forties-style *chauffeuse* chair was covered with a cherry-colored satin while the Directoire armchairs were covered with a black and white striped fabric and, in place of a headboard, Bergero painted a giant tulip.

If you venture to ask the reason for this latest change in direction, Roberto Bergero shrugs his shoulders and replies that he prefers parrots over sparrows and strong colors over a dull palette … at least for today. Because, with Roberto, you never know what tomorrow will bring.

A SEVENTEENTH-CENTURY RECONSTRUCTION

Joseph Achkar and Michel Charrière

A SEVENTEENTH-CENTURY RECONSTRUCTION

They call themselves experts of the seventeenth century and lovers of historic homes, but in reality this too short—and too modest—résumé does not do the decorators Joseph Achkar and Michel Charrière justice.

Joseph and Michel are magicians blessed with the gift of enchanting us with period reconstructions of exceptional quality. The perfect marriage of their respective talents has resulted in the completion of a number of prestigious projects, including several palaces in the Middle East, private homes and apartments in Europe and the United States, and the resurrection of the Hôtel de Gesvres, one of the most beautiful of the French capital's mansions.

Built in 1660 for Joachim Seiglières de Boisfranc—the chancellor to Monsieur, brother of the Sun King Louis XIV—the home was passed on to his son-in-law, the Duke of Gesvres. Joseph and Michel conducted thorough research, which revealed that in the nineteenth century no traces of the past splendor of the large home remained when it was converted into offices!

Joseph and Michel are true archaeologists of the past who, loyal to the spirit of the seventeenth century, recreated the entrance hall of their second home without ostentation—gray walls, no parquet or gilding, linen curtains—and reconstructed in the succeeding rooms, from the foyer to the Chamber of Mirrors, a display of wealth from the duke's time and that of his heirs with all its essential luxury. Today, the Hôtel de Gesvres's succession of rooms is full of treasures, magnificent period furniture—including a beautiful eighteenth-century *lit à la Polonaise*—delicate figurines made of biscuit porcelain, beautiful antique carpets, and silverware of outstanding quality. At the end of the enfilade, the painted paneling of the Chamber of Mirrors grabs your attention. This room was created by Claude Audran in 1680 for the statesman Antoine de Sartine, with panels painted by Watteau and Desportes. The designers discovered this masterpiece beneath thick layers of gray paint, as they did the magnificent ceiling painted by Louis de Boulogne.

Thanks to Joseph Achkar and Michel Charrière's venture, the Hôtel de Gesvres has regained its former glory and, due to their perseverance, Paris is enriched by one of the finest examples of seventeenth-century architecture.

A FUTURISTIC DESIGN LAIR

Yves and Victor Gastou

Andy Warhol

SUPER ACTION ART TOY
MAD THE PHANTOM THIEF
Casino Kitty Qee
Choco Minty
KOZIK
THE FUTURE IS STUPID
DONNA KARAN NEW YORK
THE CLASSICS
STEREOTYPE
Toxic SWAMP DOG
Toxic SWAMP DOG
SKULL
BE@RBRICK
The MANIAC
kidrobot
infantree
KNUCKLE BEAR
KNUCKLE BEAR
KOZIK
BE MY GUEST
RED MAGIC COLLECTION
TOO FAST TO LIVE
TOO YOUNG TO DIE
LIBERTY
KILLER CATZ
REACH BEAR
CARROT SHAKE JAKE
YOUNG ELSA gardener
Dalek
LeSportsac
MECHTORIANS
MECHTORIANS

What sets the antiquarian and art dealer Yves Gastou apart from his colleagues is his uncanny ability to unearth exceptional furniture and objects that will not be recognized as masterpieces by the general public until much later.

Champion of the forties style from the outset, Yves showed the work of André Arbus and Marc du Plantier in his first gallery in Paris. However, always on the lookout for new aesthetic challenges, he subsequently turned his attention to the designs of the Memphis Group and the amazing furniture and products created by Ettore Sottsass, Andrea Branzi, Matteo Thun, Michael Graves, and Michele De Lucchi.

When he moved his gallery to rue Bonaparte, Gastou daringly entrusted the "look" of his new space to Sottsass, displaying pieces by André Dubreuil, Mark Brazier-Jones, Gilbert Poillerat, and Maria Pergay in its windows and organizing exhibits showcasing furniture designed by Philippe Hiquily and Ado Chale. These days it is no surprise that he is passionate about Hollywood, Walt Disney characters, comic strips, and Japanese manga because it was always clear that any new interest of his would be taken up by other collectors.

When Yves takes a liking to a particular style or designer, he becomes completely engrossed in their work. When he decided to move into a new apartment on the quai Malaquais, he filled the space at an alarming rate with everything relating to the imaginary world of comic books, together with anything fantastic, exceptional, and unusual that he could find on this subject.

Like any other native of the South of France, Yves has a sense of humor without necessarily taking himself too seriously. He also readily admits that he has created "a childish world filled with toys like a child's room, but all the items are works of art that will one day be recognized as important works."

Yves Gastou's apartment is a visual shock, a place where the strange and unusual prevail. It is a unique place where one is thrown into a bizarre and hallucinogenic take on childhood. However, it is also an art mecca filled with objects that—today—may seem trivial, meaningless, and unimportant, but no doubt will be argued over in a few decades by the big design collectors. Once again, Yves Gastou will have led the way.

A CONTEMPORARY URBAN PIED-À-TERRE

Jacques Garcia

Ton sombre éclat est prostitution, crabe sublime

prostitution
crabe sublime

A CONTEMPORARY URBAN PIED-À-TERRE

The style of the famous French designer Jacques Garcia is associated with lavishly furnished interior spaces, imposing mansions, and luxury hotels, where everything is, or seems, authentic. Simply listing his most noted creations—Hôtel Costes in Paris, the Château de Menou, his own Château du Champ-de-Bataille, and Hôtel Mansart de Sagonne in Paris's Marais district—is enough to recognize the value of his exceptional talent.

Garcia would certainly take exception to our accusing him of trickery. Brilliant trickery, of course. How else could you describe the interiors that he seems to pull out of his hat with the ease of a magician, which appear to come straight from the seventeenth, eighteenth, and nineteenth centuries? So, imagine our surprise when, out of the blue, he announced that, during the week, he would be living in a pied-à-terre near the Palais Royal, and that he would be giving his new home a completely twenty-first-century design makeover!

For his new urban residence, Garcia was determined to break with his past. What could be more fitting for a man with an overloaded schedule, who can crash in the splendor of his Normandy château every weekend, and who, during weekdays, seeks a certain "visual calm"? That's why this time he chose a resolutely contemporary style with a classical accent here and there, together with the added impact of modern artwork and ethnic collectibles.

In Garcia's new apartment, the contrast between different cultures is clearly discernible. This rationale is established upon entry by a pair of dressers decorated in silver leaf, the flooring made of large squares of oxidized bronze, and two prehistoric concretions. In the living room, visitors find silver-leafed accordion doors that reach up to the ceiling, constructivist-style bookcases, and a series of decorative stools with clawed bronze legs, which all express—like the rest of the furniture: sofas, decorative tables, armchairs, and chairs—the fertile imagination of their owner.

Creativity has never been lacking for Jacques Garcia. Once again he has succeeded brilliantly in creating an intimate space, despite the overwhelming presence of furniture, artwork, and various objects, each one more original than the next—such as the cast aluminum "cloud ceiling," which replaces the ubiquitous classic chandelier, whose numerous oil lamps create at night a diffused light full of atmosphere.

Garcia's personality is attractive because he doesn't take himself seriously and rejects any form of pretention. Here is a world-famous man, whom history will recognize as one of the leading designers of his time, and yet he speaks of his work with humor and a hint of frivolity. On a Sunday evening, after a weekend of dinners and revelry in Champ-de-Bataille, we picture him at ease, separating himself from anything glamorous, and it is quite easy to imagine him in his comfortable bedroom hung with dark brown fabric, reading a book or listening to soft music. There is no doubt about it: Garcia epitomizes a unique combination of aesthetic judgment, originality, and sense of well-being—but, then, we already knew that.

ECLECTIC GRANDEUR

MANTEGNA

CHEF-
D'OEUVRE
MANTEGNA

ECLECTIC GRANDEUR

First there was the prestigious address: a quiet street lined with town houses and luxury apartment buildings behind the Arc de Triomphe—known by Parisians as the Etoile (meaning "star" and describing the point where twelve roads converge). Then there was the apartment itself with its spacious rooms, stunning high ceilings, and eighteenth-century wood paneling that had been installed long ago by the legendary Maison Jansen design firm. There was also the meticulous restoration and infectious enthusiasm of architect Serge Donnard, and gallery owner Yves Gastou's specialist input concerning decor, artwork, and furniture. Added to this heady mix it might be worth mentioning that for the collector clients it was love at first sight and that, having eventually bought the apartment, they applaud themselves every day for having surrendered to temptation.

Certain places show off their grandeur and this is undeniably true in the case of this apartment. No one can enter the living room without falling under the spell of its large proportions, or without being overwhelmed by the spherical chandelier, consisting of interlaced rings, created specially for the space by Hubert le Gall. Or without being enchanted by the André-Charles Boulle armoire, the Marc Held vintage chair with zebra-patterned upholstery, the brass and acrylic chair created by the sculptor Philippe Hiquily, or the black lacquer furniture, which bears the signature of Jean-Charles Moreux, a legend of forties style.

Here there is no question of snobbery or of merely putting together a collection of well-known "names" and references, but the owners' intuitive need to surround themselves with all that is beautiful and rare. They have closely followed Yves Gastou's advice and unconventional aesthetic process, not thinking twice about creating unusual "marriages" between various periods and styles, juxtaposing, for instance, Alain Jacquet's *La Vague* (1970) with an eighteenth-century terra-cotta bust, a pair of classic consoles by Jansen with a Jacques Villeglé artwork or a seventies brass-framed, velvet-cushioned sofa.

However, the focal point of this incredible design is, without a doubt, the furnishings that have been chosen for the bedroom. Almost the entire space is occupied by a monumental bed, accented by an eight-part folding screen. The black and gold lacquered bed, embellished with rock crystal fragments, is an extraordinary piece of work by Hubert le Gall. The acutely refined decor continues in the bathroom with its walls embedded with mother-of-pearl and a table created in the seventies by Jacques Duval-Brasseur. This is a place where boldness and well-established taste merge harmoniously!

AN EIGHTEENTH-CENTURY ARTISTIC DWELLING

The Musée Nissim de Camondo

AN EIGHTEENTH-CENTURY ARTISTIC DWELLING

In 1911, Count Moïse de Camondo (1860–1935), born into a wealthy Turkish banking dynasty, commissioned the architect René Sergent to build a mansion on rue de Monceau, modeled after the Petit Trianon in Versailles, to house his fabulous collection of furniture and objets d'art.

Camondo nurtured a true passion for the decorative arts of the eighteenth century. For over half a century he bought cabinetry masterpieces in sales from the most important art collectors, in addition to more ordinary pieces to serve as a backdrop for his fine acquisitions. In the spring of 1914 the count hosted a series of functions during which guests were dazzled by the elegant architecture of the building and its imposing entrance hall, the stone staircase adorned with a beautiful wrought iron railing—a replica of one in a Toulouse mansion. Wandering through the luxurious parlors, the visitors discovered, among other wonders, beautiful cylinder secretaries, dressers, writing desks, and tables created by the likes of Jean-Baptiste-Claude Sené, Jean-François Oeben, Jean-Henri Riesener, and Bernard van Riesen Burgh. Also, carpets and screens by the Savonnerie Manufactory, Louis XVI girandoles and wall clocks, porcelain from Sèvres and Meissen, Aubusson tapestries representing *The Fables of La Fontaine*, the beautiful *Bacchante* painted by Elisabeth-Louise Vigée Le Brun, and an oak-shelf–paneled library full of old, red morocco leather-bound books.

Camondo lived in this incredible dwelling until his death on November 14, 1935. Shattered by the death of his son, Nissim, who was killed in aerial combat on September 5, 1917, he decided to bequeath his home and collection to the Union Centrale des Arts Décoratifs and, in December 1936, the Musée Nissim de Camondo was inaugurated and opened to the public. Compliant with his wishes, nothing was to be changed in this "perfect reconstruction of an eighteenth-century artistic dwelling," which prevented the installation of handrails and required that his father's portrait and a photograph of his son be on permanent display. As a precaution, in 1939 the museum was emptied of all its contents, the collection, transported to the Château de Valençay, barely escaped the fire started by the Second SS Division. Moïse's daughter, Beatrice, her husband Léon Reinach, and their children, Fanny and Bertrand, were deported to Drancy and then to Auschwitz-Birkenau. Beatrice succumbed to the harsh torture of the concentration camp in 1945, two weeks before the forced evacuation of the camp and following the deaths of her children and her husband.

Today, the Musée Nissim de Camondo is an undeniable statement of both the exceptional quality of its collection of eighteenth-century decorative art and of the way of living at the beginning of the twentieth century—aside from the collection, visitors can admire the luxurious and "modern" kitchens and bathrooms of the era, which reflect the essential need for comfort of a beauty-hungry aesthete.

LIGHT AND WHIMSICAL

Florence Dostal

LIGHT AND WHIMSICAL

The photographer Florence Dostal was born in France, but her childhood was spent in sunny California, where she fell madly in love with the American way of life, Hollywood, Mickey Mouse, and Donald Duck. When she returned to France, the young girl filled her baggage with the glamour and cheer of her adopted country.

Florence is a real businesswoman. At only eighteen she founded her own company, called Achille, creating chic and flamboyant unisex novelty socks. A few decades later, after selling her business, she made a name for herself as a photographer of animals.

Witty, spiritual, and tinged with irony, Florence's style is surprising. Her first apartment in Montparnasse had pink walls, a Folies Bergère–style wrought iron staircase, and furniture based on the cartoons of her favorite character, Mickey Mouse. However, when the apartment above the famous Le Dôme restaurant became available she snapped it up, not hesitating to rearrange the conventional space, dating back to 1897, by painting it all white and filling it with stuffed animals and designer furniture.

Small, cute, full of life, and always followed by Toto, her faithful Jack Russell terrier, Florence has always given her imagination free reign. Today, when we enter her home for the first time, it is astounding to note the skill with which she has combined white walls and almost all white furniture. Simply walking around the kitchen accented with brushed steel fittings, light muslin drapes, and snazzy crystal chandeliers is enough to realize that the space is full of original ideas. Florence Dostal knows how to decorate a room with Marc Newson leather chairs and geometric Verner Panton curtains. She creates the most alluring bedroom around a white bed, pristine with a pure white muslin screen. Florence embellishes her white stucco Napoleon III dining room with a huge stuffed dog, a baroque mirror, and a table and chairs designed by Ross Lovegrove. She made the most of the bathroom's potential by contracting an artisan, who, over the course of a few weeks, decorated the walls with a mosaïc by Pierre Mesguich tracing the branches of a weeping willow. Even the lavatory, an archetypally intimate place, has not escaped her creative fever. As a pièce de résistance, she created Absinthe Green stucco walls, embedded with an impressive number of glass lenses.

Because humor and originality are fundamental features of her style, Florence Dostal daringly reupholstered a sixties chair with Emilio Pucci fabric and scattered stuffed animals around her apartment: a deer, a duck, a seagull, a Saint Bernard, and a Labrador. Her menagerie of animals makes the peaceful haven above Le Dôme one of the most original and imaginative spaces in the capital.

A RUSSIAN DACHA IN PARIS

Didier Rabes

A RUSSIAN DACHA IN PARIS

A Petit Trianon in the suburbs? A Moroccan lounge on the top floor of a New York skyscraper? A Russian dacha in the attic of a Parisian town house? Why not? Especially if Didier Rabes, an outstanding designer who has the rare gift of creating unexpected and unusual interiors, is appointed to the job.

Didier's portfolio of work includes the ground floor of a palatial building on rue de Rivoli designed by the great neoclassicists Percier and Fontaine, and one floor of an eighteenth-century château near Chantilly—the château in which Madame de Staël and Benjamin Constant conducted their love affair. In both he has managed, with his customary panache, to create the perfect illusion of a period setting.

Having established his new office on rue Saint-Honoré on the top floor of the former Hôtel de Noailles, Didier did not hesitate to incorporate the garrets—a maze of small rooms with sloping ceilings—into this unique dreamlike place. An exotic dream, inspired by his many trips to Central Europe, Russia, where Didier was particularly captivated by the unaffected beauty of the dacha.

Nearly a year of work and the assistance of a brilliant carpenter were needed for the attic of the Hôtel de Noailles to be transformed into a place worthy of a Chekhov short story. Blond wood logs covering the walls, pitch-pine flooring and doors, and many "authentic" details, such as the fretted wood balustrade, are designed to transport dazzled visitors to faraway Russia.

For the decor, Didier chose charming objects and modes of display that truly capture the countryside ambiance of traditional cottages. Walls mounted with hunting trophies, "cottage style" tables and chairs, wine-colored sofas and *chauffeuse* chairs—protected by white canvas covers during the summer—copper sconces and candelabras, an old rustic wardrobe filled with collectibles, together with some elegant touches, like the eighteenth-century chaise and a Louis XVI medallion, once again demonstrate the remarkable talent of the master of the house.

THE BESPOKE HOME

Pierre Yovanovitch

The achievements of the French interior designer Pierre Yovanovitch could be compared to the chalk-stripe pattern of a bespoke suit, made by a London Savile Row tailor, because the name Yovanovitch is inextricably linked to perfection.

Smooth walls and paneling, rare wood, vintage furniture, brilliantly polished marble … his style is recognizable at first glance, and it was inevitable that Pierre would sooner or later find himself in one of these majestic Parisian apartment buildings on the Left Bank, whose tall windows provide exceptional views of the place de la Concorde.

The original version of this apartment, with a surface area of several thousand square feet, was, according to Pierre, "one hundred percent *vieille* France" and therefore very disturbing for someone like him who has a penchant for the reconstruction of historical styles. He keeps both feet firmly rooted in reality and has been passionate about twentieth-century Swedish design for many years.

Therefore, the following was inevitable: walls demolished, the entrance fitted with a white and black marble floor, a square dining room transformed into a round dining room, entirely refurbished and redecorated bathrooms, a modernized kitchen, and windows replaced by a panoramic glass wall that now frames one of the most famous of Paris's sights.

Yovanovitch was very careful to not make his interior space a showroom. Within his new environment he has assembled a collection of vintage furniture, including a coral-lacquered Gunnar Asplund piano, chairs by Frank Lloyd Wright, cast-iron benches by Folke Benson, gilded ceramic bowls by Olof Hult, and a splendid writing desk by Carl Malmsten. The result is an elegant and welcoming apartment that provides the occupant with a sense of comfort and security, while illustrating his belief that living surrounded by masterpieces and rare furniture is an art in itself. At Yovanovitch's home, you can touch the piano keys, relax on the fifties sofa by Edward Wormley, and eat at the Philippe Jean table, sitting on a Joseph-André Motte chair.

"Here, we aren't at the Musée des Arts Décoratifs or the Louvre," says the designer. "They are on the opposite side, on the other bank of the Seine."

A BAROQUE FANTASY

Gérard Trémolet

POUR

A BAROQUE FANTASY

As far as interior decoration is concerned, former fashion designer Gérard Trémolet, to whom minimalism is an anathema, swears by the exuberance of the baroque style. He finds it viscerally impossible to live without piles of furniture and miscellaneous objects, and without the crazy disorder that makes his apartment, in the shadow of the Gare du Nord, one of the most original spaces in the capital.

Trémolet worked for many years as a stylist for Lesage, the famous embroidery house, which explains the haute couture quality seen in his home. He has an irrepressible urge to drape the windows with avalanches of fabric and heavy trimmings, cover his sofa cushions with fur or luxurious brocade, decorate the walls with large two-tone stripes, and furnish his bed with a canopy and silk damask curtains.

Trémolet smiles thinly when you use the word "decadent" to describe his home on the first floor of a Haussmann building. What matters to him is the theatrical effect of a niche displaying a marble bust version of the Apollo Belvedere, a pair of Garouste and Bonetti chairs covered with faux leopard fabric, and a gilt-bronze candelabra topped with multicolored shades. Could Gérard's style be described as "tawdry" or "artificial"? Not at all. Trémolet has an innate sense of chicness—and he knows it—with no "cheap" effects evident in his apartment. This is epitomized by the double door that he has embellished with beautiful rococo arabesques, a wall painted Etruscan Red on which are mounted gilded consoles housing exotic porcelain "knickknacks" found in the Chinese shops of the 14th arrondissement, and a luxurious Louis XV sofa worthy of a royal favorite.

In Trémolet's home, "red is in," his favorite color and its many variants exploding everywhere—in his choice of fabrics, on the walls, and even on the refrigerator in the kitchen. A rustic kitchen that evokes elements found in a country home and where Gérard prepares food as refined as his interior decoration.

Jean Cocteau had a distinct predilection for the dramatic and called this condition "my red and gold illness." Gérard Trémolet has the good fortune of suffering from this syndrome too, his fever creating a remarkably original "wild" style.

A MONOCHROMATIC MASTERPIECE

by Chahan Minassian

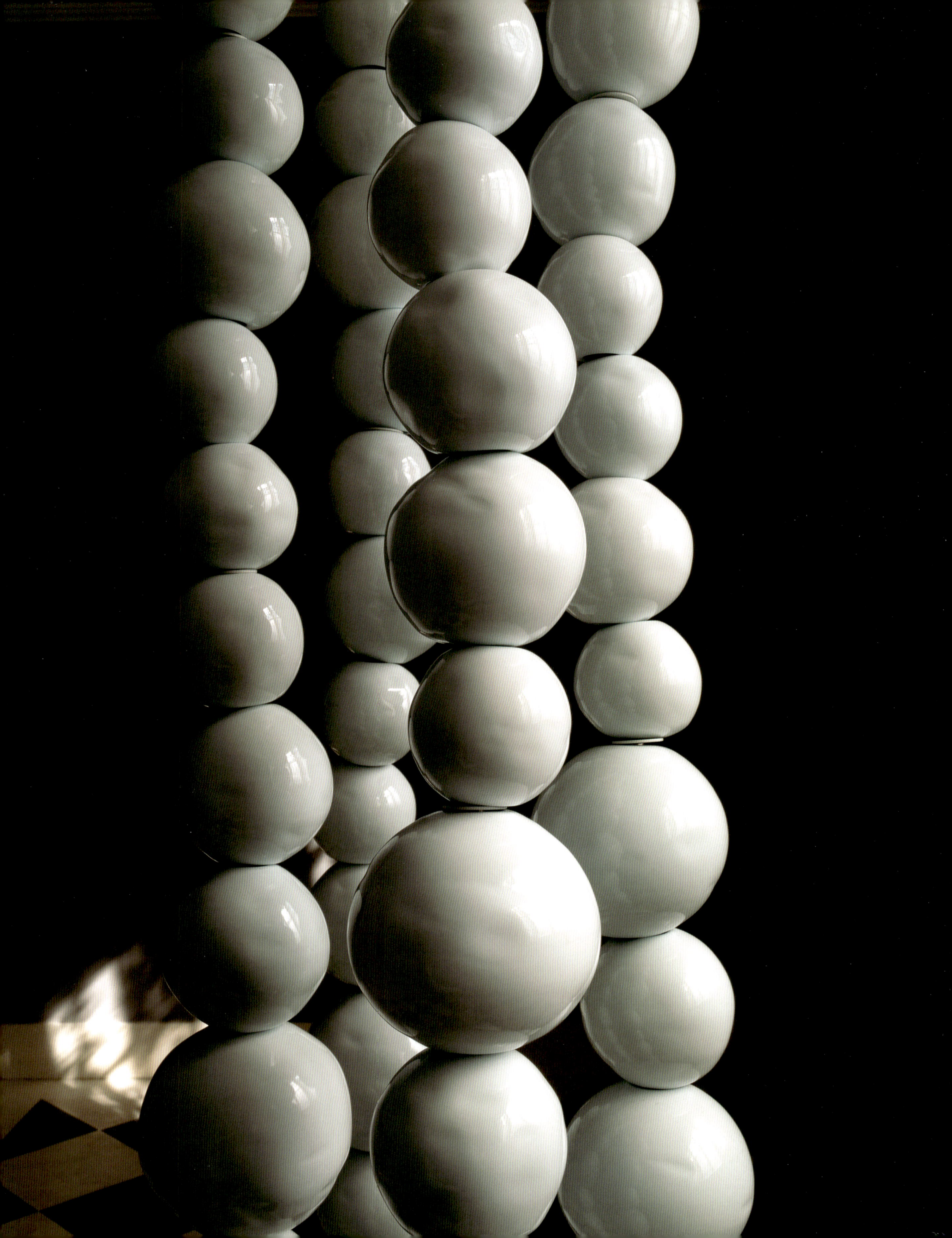

che ou sublime ?

DE L'A.C.T.
du 5 octobre au 2
patients
STONE
BILLY PRESTON
RTL
mercredi 17oct. 21h
HEBEY
THÉAT
octobre
FAUST
la tragique histoire
et la fin lamentable
du DOCTEUR FAUST
carré
21h
la soirée
DE BETHUNE
D'ERLON

A MONOCHROMATIC MASTERPIECE

Chahan Minassian's last name indicates exotic origins, but this does not mean that the interior designer, born in Lebanon and of Armenian descent, creates spaces punctuated by Middle Eastern baroque accents.

Ever since his youth, Chahan has been completely faithful to the principles of Le Corbusier and Mies van der Rohe. Faced with the incontrovertible "less is more" notion of Mies, we note that Minassian's simple creations are primarily distinguished by an unusually neutral palette and an unconditional obsession with quality, from which the designer never deviates when selecting artwork, furniture, and other decorative objects.

Minassian does not shy away from large and complex transformation projects, as is evidenced by his many private schemes in France and the United States. One of his latest works is the refurbishment of an early twentieth-century home on the elegant rue de Lille for a property developer and art collector. This proved to be particularly difficult—due to the presence of a spiral staircase that literally seems suspended in midair—costing him many sleepless nights. We can say without exaggeration that the designer conceived, within the framework of the existing facade, a completely new house, whose decor features a minimalist approach, delicate, almost monochromatic colors, and an array of unusual materials. A kidney-shaped sofa, straight out of the fifties, by Vladimir Kagan, a white mantel inlaid with pebbles, a diptych by Sophie Calle, a chair designed by Paul Mathieu, and a ceramic bowl by Pamela Sunday are typical of the Minassian style. Although so many choices were carefully weighed, they were not ultimately critical to the overall success of the design and cannot compete with the fact that, after a while, one feels like one is strolling through a three-dimensional black-and-white photograph. A unique experience that reflects the decisive personality and remarkable individuality of an interior designer who, with the incredibly enthusiastic support of his client, took up a risky challenge: to create an original and staggering design within an empty shell.

REFINED BOHEMIA

Gavin McKinley

JEAN DUNAND
PIERRE CHAR
J.H PIERNEEF
The New SCULPTURE
Sièges africains
FANG
mondrian
EILEEN GRAY
EARLY ANCIENT GLASS
ペルシアのガラス
ペルシアの古陶器
エジプトの古代ガラス
BRAZIL
Legendary AFRICA

ANDRE NAUDÉ

REFINED BOHEMIA

The late New Zealand art dealer Gavin McKinley lived in a typical artist's studio behind the place des Ternes. A tall and open space with a mezzanine floor, it included a bedroom, a small bathroom, and a tiny kitchen in which his impressive cooking skills and encyclopedic knowledge of art went hand in hand.

An amateur photographer of "artistic nudes," Gavin McKinley did not like contemporary art. He displayed a rather dry sense of humor and developed a particular passion for the work of the English painter and sculptor Glyn Philpot. Thanks to McKinley, we discovered the fascinating work of this aesthete, a favorite of English high society, who immortalized—all with the same ease—society ladies, jazz musicians, boxers, and beautiful young black men. It is also through McKinley that we discovered how to live in an artist's studio in an atmosphere that is both bohemian and refined.

McKinley claimed he did not like decoration and preferred "organized chaos." What he forgot to mention is that his innate sense of aesthetics allowed him to combine works by Philpot with empty antique frames, eighteenth-century sofas, a library full of art books, a pair of boxing gloves, an old Spanish chest, and valuable antiques, without committing the slightest error in taste. In his home a beautiful portrait of Philpot's little niece was propped on an easel next to a piece of art deco dining room furniture, a blatantly erotic drawing, and a plaster statue of Adonis, without causing any visual discomfort. It didn't take long to realize that this man who hungered for beauty and ran the auction rooms with a frenzy similar to that described by Paul Morand in *L'Homme pressé*, who managed to divide his time between his homes in Paris, New Zealand, Australia, and London with the precision of a Swiss watch, who prepared a delicious Bœuf Bourguignon in his cramped kitchenette with the practice of a great chef, and who unearthed treasures in the back rooms of country antique shops, was in fact an extraordinary human being and a one-of-a-kind aesthete.

Gavin McKinley left this life reluctantly, because he still had "a thousand things to do." It is unknown what became of the artist's studio and its contents; and, as is often the case, only a few photographs remain to evoke the portrait of an unforgettable man and his interior.

A COLLECTOR'S RETREAT

"I acquired these objects through chance meetings and during my travels," comments the resident who chose to live surrounded by his collections in a loft, behind the Palais Royal, nestled in the yard of an eighteenth-century town house that opens its doors only to a select few.

A lover of the beautiful and rare, his large loft is an extraordinary space in which he jealously guards his furniture, objets d'art, and paintings that have been selected with a remarkable talent for evoking a stage-like setting.

His profound knowledge and relationship with the art and antique worlds are the basis of his taste for eclectic and diverse objects. This explains why he did not think twice about combining the Empire style with forties designs and contemporary art with old paintings. To access this large living space, where iron columns reveal an industrial past, we ascend a staircase whose walls are decorated with forties-style shell appliqués designed by Jean-Charles Moreux. Further along, in a vast area flooded with light, the eye is immediately captivated by a chaise longue, created in 1982 by Pucci De Rossi, and a portrait of a woman painted by Eugène Huc in 1927, whose title—*Simplicity*—is as unexpected as the place that houses it.

In examining how the master of the house has arranged a particular piece of furniture or painting, for instance, *Nu aux fleurs* (Nude with flowers)—a 1950 painting by the painter and photographer Pierre Molinier—and a futuristic, sparkling, cabochon-encrusted sofa by the late Marco de Gueltzl, one understands his natural love of decorating and his fondness for bold juxtaposition. This approach is also evident in the fusion of a portrait of the Maharaja of Kapurthala hanging against a pleated fabric wall covering behind a magnificent Empire bed, a Chesterfield-like armchair by Philippe Starck, and the original *Puzzle* nightclub seat designed by Guillaume Castel—which quietly cohabitates with a bronze sculpture by Antoine Bourdelle, and drawings and paintings by Keith Haring, Pierre Alechinsky, Jean-Michel Basquiat, and Amédée Ozenfant.

A "mix and match" triumph of our time? Definitely. But, moreover, an extraordinary collection united with a unique space—a total vision that will long remain etched in our memories.

AN ELEGANT FAMILY HAVEN

Bénédicte and Jean-Jacques Wattel

LA SEÑORA
PETIT MUSÉE

Mythes GRECS

AN ELEGANT FAMILY HAVEN

London has its mews and Paris has its villas—private and secluded streets where those who can afford to can stay hidden in a country village atmosphere that offers the illusion of living far from the city. Just blocks from the Arc de Triomphe, the Villa Saïd, once the residence of such luminaries as Pierre Louÿs, Arthur Rubinstein, and—more recently—Charles Aznavour, is now home to Bénédicte and Jean-Jacques Wattel. This couple, experts in furniture and auctions, discovered the villa a decade ago, before settling with their children in its deceptively large duplex.

The Wattels began their careers as directors of Manufacture Saint-Jean in Aubusson. Not satisfied in merely making, reproducing, and restoring their world-famous tapestries, they forged an international reputation in the interior decorating and design field by commissioning great furniture designers, like Elizabeth Garouste and Mattia Bonetti, to come up with designs that incorporated Aubusson's work. Following the success of their collection, the Wattels decided that the time was right to "move up" to Paris, where in the Villa Saïd they found the ideal haven for their family and collection of decorative art.

For a long time now, Jean-Jacques has had a passion for the outstanding work of twentieth-century French ceramists. In contrast, Bénédicte is obsessed by vintage haute couture from the same period and extravagant costume jewelry. It's not really surprising that a couple of dedicated connoisseurs live in a space worthy of their acquisitions, with everything that surrounds them being part of a visually enchanting environment.

The impressive high ceilings and overhanging mezzanine grant the Wattels a dramatic backdrop for showcasing a large Gérard Garouste tapestry, a beautiful Aubusson rug, an eighteenth-century terra-cotta statue, Empire furniture, pieces by Garouste and Bonetti, and a collection of ceramic art from the first half of the last century. It all comes together to form an overall sense of great elegance that reflects the taste of the owners. At the Wattels, one searches in vain for easy, predictable, and reassuring "deco," instead being captivated throughout by attention to originality and willingness to please and surprise. Bénédicte and Jean-Jacques do not care about what's considered trendy or à la mode. They love the beautiful and rare, period. And they cultivate, with remarkable tenacity, the art of well-being within an extraordinary setting and location.

A LESSON IN STYLE

by Guy Thodoroff

OSSIAN

HOMMAGE
A
MADEMOISELLE
DE BEAUJOUR

A LESSON IN STYLE

For most of those who live or want to live in Paris, the prospect of living in a duplex measuring almost five thousand square feet and overlooking the Champs de Mars is an unattainable dream. It is true that few of us can afford the luxury of a magnificent eagle's nest with views over our neighbors' gardens and towards the slender silhouette of the Eiffel Tower. But for the clients who asked the French designer Guy Thodoroff to fulfill their dreams by creating the ultimate interior decoration perfect for their needs, the sky was the limit.

The designer's dream client is somebody who does not dwell on the size of the budget or the extent of the work and utters the magic words: "carte blanche!" Throughout his career, Thodoroff has had the privilege of dealing only with such clients and of being able to decorate without the slightest obstacle to his ideas and creativity, as if he were working on his own home. He has completed many prestigious projects in France and abroad, but as his customers prefer to avoid the limelight, Guy and his projects have followed their example by voluntarily withdrawing into the shadows. For the designer and his clients, discretion automatically doubles exclusivity—the interior of the duplex near the Champs de Mars reflects this philosophy.

However, it is hard not to gawk at an entry covered in emerald velvet like a precious jewelry box and adorned with niches displaying a pair of eighteenth-century terra-cotta statues of Eastern figures. It is even harder not to fall in love with the French furniture and bronze work that would not be out of place in the greatest museums. And how can one not be dazzled by the gueridon table designed by Andrey Voronikhin and paintings of outstanding beauty?

Thodoroff dressed the sofas, chairs, and walls of the duplex with materials suited to the understated luxury that pervades the space—silk, velvet, marble—and his lesson in style reminds us of a time when designers only dreamed of quality, and magazines for connoisseurs, like *Connaissance des Arts*, featured interiors where aesthetic judgment met splendor and rarity. Thodoroff's latest achievement is a brilliant testament, proving that he undeniably belongs to this rich period.

SWEDISH STYLE IN PARIS

Katinka de Montal

SWEDISH STYLE IN PARIS

Katinka de Montal, decorator and jewelry designer, had retained a vivid memory of her native Sweden—particularly of her grandmother's eighteenth-century manor house in Ållonö—and a distinct taste for northern light, crystal chandeliers, and Gustavian furniture. Finding a home as peaceful as those reflected in the quiet lakes around Stockholm was nothing short of a miracle. However, Katinka is not easily discouraged and she eventually found an abandoned orangery, overlooking the garden of a Saint-Germain town house, which seemed entirely appropriate for transformation into a real herrgård.

It was not an easy task. Katinka was compelled to excavate the site to increase ceiling height, evacuate tons of earth, enlarge windows, create glass doors leading to the garden and—above all else—address the concerns of the neighbors who feared the worst. They felt as if their lovely paved courtyard, adorned with a statue of Terpsichore inspired by that of Antonio Canova, was threatened by this energetic Swede. Katinka needed to channel all of her diplomacy to convince them that she was not an iconoclast!

What they did not know is that their new neighbor had no problem mounting a ladder herself—in an apron or in an haute couture dress—to paint clouds on the ceiling, to decorate remolded walls with an ivy trellis and gold-leaf garland, to apply a faux marble effect to medallions and plaster columns, or to hang eighteenth-century–style chandeliers that she had made from bronze armatures and crystals found at the Saint-Ouen–Porte de Clignancourt flea market.

Of course, Katinka's "orangery" had some help from other designers and contractors. Her friend, the artist Joy de Rohan Chabot, made her mark on a pair of footrests and a wrought iron railing embellished with leaves, birds, and butterflies. At the famous Saint-Pierre market, she found fabric to upholster the sofas, chairs, and the gueridon table in the dining room. A plasterer decorated the entry doors with neoclassical stucco urns and, to give the interior a touch of authenticity, Katinka added gilt-bronze candlesticks and antiques that she had inherited from her family.

Katinka had finally recreated her childhood home and the neighbors were no longer worried; irrefutable success.

THE EPITOME OF CHIC

Patrick Fourtin

INDIEN
GLOBE
Physique Politique Historique
J. FOREST
PARIS

THE EPITOME OF CHIC

Paris is full of secret places and even those who know the city like the back of their hand discover a new hideaway every day. Gardens in the middle of a block and shaded by ancient trees, artists' studios perched atop buildings like eagles' nests, and courtyards resembling informal country gardens. All this adds to the pleasure of discovering a life hidden between the capital's streets and avenues; and since the antiques collector Patrick Fourtin has a knack for finding the extraordinary, he seized the opportunity to move into one of these little-known courtyard buildings.

In reality, the term "antiques collector" does not do Fourtin justice because he is much more than that and does not correspond to the stereotype at all. Fourtin is really an aesthete whose daily life is marked by the pursuit of beauty, whether it is found in a cabinet, table, vase, chair, or lamp—as long as the object that catches his eye is exceptional and intriguing in its originality, novelty, or boldness of its form. Due to his insatiable passion for the decorative arts and the work of great twentieth-century artists, as well as his following of everything happening today in the field of design, Patrick's Paris gallery has become the hot spot for those who seek out the remarkable.

His private life as secret as the place in which he lives, Fourtin opens his door to only a select few. Delighted are those who are admitted into the "Holy of Holies," which is made up of several small rooms where Fourtin has used his objects to create real "artwork," their limited number manifesting his selective mind. The artifacts include, among others, a beautiful chaise longue; chairs by André Arbus; a large Greek vase; a plaster head depicting Juno; a forties-style table; a beautiful antique male torso; and mirrors, low tables, and lamps chosen for the elegance and refinement of their form. Elegance and refinement: two words that are at the heart of Patrick Fourtin's aesthetic approach and that make his ivory tower on the slopes of Montmartre a unique visual experience.

AN ANTIQUARIAN'S DELIGHT

Olivier Trebosc and Alfred van Lelyveld

Sarah Sherburne –

Olivier Trebosc and Alfred van Lelyveld are a Franco-Dutch duo who once owned antique shops in Amsterdam and New York, but were then seduced by the City of Light and began looking for an apartment in Paris suited to their needs. An unexpected development: after moving into a turn of the century building on boulevard Berthier—"a house once built for a concubine," adds Trebosc, originally from Narbonne—they fell for the first floor of a building just steps from the Opéra.

Trebosc and van Lelyveld, who are not—far from it—ordinary antiquarians, are firmly convinced that it is absurd to collect antiques if the furniture, objects, and paintings are not to be showcased in an interior that is in perfect harmony with its contents; an authentic interior, down to even the minutest of details, and exuding a certain grandeur. In other words, no museum-quality Louis XVI furniture in a rustic cottage or an art deco villa. And no eighteenth-century portrait collections in a contemporary building made of concrete, glass, and steel. Trebosc and van Lelyveld advocate integrating an antiques collection within the total re-creation of an era: a time warp and complete illusion such as the famous French designer Jacques Garcia regularly fabricates with so much ease. And so it was that Olivier and Alfred, avid admirers of the work of Garcia, whom they befriended, entrusted Jacques and his continuous stream of brilliant ideas with the comprehensive overhaul of their new home.

Today, the space no longer reflects the dismal aspect in which its occupants found it. Garcia has supported and advised the couple, sketching out plans on the bare walls, and suggesting that they add an unassuming entrance hall and a dining room with an antique marble floor that would not look out of place in a stately room. The awkward partitions were removed and, strange as it may seem, the "new" has gradually given way to … the "old"!

Alfred and Olivier's apartment can be described without hesitation as a masterpiece, because what Garcia and his clients have done borders on the unbelievable. Faced with this sublime tour de force, nobody, really nobody, could imagine that the eighteenth-century paneling, originally from the United States, had long been collecting dust in Trebosc and van Lelyveld's warehouse before finding its place here. It is the same for the entrance, fit for a palace, and for the bedroom with its Louis XVI canopy bed, the deceptively accurate Directoire-style bathroom, and the dining room where—the ultimate decadence—a beautiful Louis XV *lit à la Polonaise* has been installed. What was once a dilapidated office space has become an authentic "château" with an apparently immutable decor. Undoubtedly this is because Jacques and his devotees did not hold back from cutting to size Gobelins tapestries to cover the entrance hall walls or ripping apart cushions to reupholster eighteenth-century wing chairs, only respecting what was just slightly damaged or had an unusual finish.

As a result, the apartment of the "antiquarians"—who specialize in sculpture from the seventeenth, eighteenth, and nineteenth centuries—may be regarded as a shining example of how to go back in time without creating pastiche. This space proves that, even in interior design, nothing can prevent an ugly duckling from metamorphosing into a beautiful swan.

6

Detail of an opulent silk curtain in the Grand Bureau of the Musée Nissim de Camondo.

8

Detail of a sofa in the Grand Bureau of the Musée Nissim de Camondo.

11

On the bottom step of the staircase sit the gold leather boots that belonged to the man who was nicknamed "The Godfather of Soul" and "Mr. Dynamite": singer and songwriter James Brown (1933–2006).

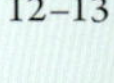

12–13

In the striking entrance hall, dramatically lit by a skylight, a beautiful Louis XV–style staircase with an elegant wrought iron railing leads to the single upstairs floor. The painting is by Jean-Michel Basquiat (1960–1988), the Plexiglas grand piano is by Schimmel, and the ottoman is by Kravitz Design, Inc. (KDI).

14

A view of the large living room with its chandelier made entirely of Swarovski crystals and an ottoman, both by KDI. The coffee table by Gabriella Crespi (b. 1922), the white leather sixties-style sofas designed for Ligne Roset by Michel Ducaroy (1925–2009), a pair of resin elephant tusks by Bartholo Pucci Collection, and–displayed on the mantelpiece–Muhammad Ali's boxing gloves and boots complete the decor.

15

In the library, Lenny's Grammy Awards are lined up on the mantelpiece. The portrait of John Lennon is by Richard Avedon (1923–2004).

16

The eighteenth-century-style woodwork in the dining room was painted a chocolate brown. The lacquered table and *klismos* chairs are vintage furniture by Karl Springer (1931–1991). A portrait of Lenny's maternal grandfather basks in the glow of a chandelier and candelabras by Baccarat.

17

Opposite the staircase, KDI placed black lacquered chairs designed by Massimo Vignelli for Stendig (c. 1970). On the resin and chrome coffee table (1970), there is a seventies light fitting representing a woman's torso. The large mirror is by KDI, the crystal sconces are by Baccarat, and the photographs are by Weegee (on the left) and Gordon Parks (on the right, behind the light).

18

In the master bedroom, the monumental polished steel bed is by KDI. There is also an Elda chair (created in 1963–65 by Joe Colombo for Comfort), a portrait of the great American soprano Leontyne Price (b. 1927) from the fifties, a resin and bronze console (c. 1960) by Paul Evans, and a chandelier and sconces by Baccarat. The Shagtastic carpet is from Unique Carpets Ltd.

19

In the bathroom, with its "noir St. Laurent" marble floor and white Calcutta marble walls, Kravitz has installed a large glass-enclosed shower, outfitted with a pair of marble benches. The gold carved wood seat is by Pedro Friedeberg (b. 1936).

20

In his dressing room, Lenny Kravitz respectfully displays his collection of stage costumes worn by celebrated predecessors such as Jimi Hendrix (1942–1970), John Lennon (1940–1980), Bob Marley (1945–1981) and Miles Davis (1926–1991). A collection of boots worn by the "hardest working man in show business," James Brown (1933–2006), is artfully displayed on the floor.

23

On the landing of the stairs leading to his apartment, Jean-Luc Gaüzère has installed an eighteenth-century marble bust and a pair of nineteenth-century ivory-inlaid chairs imported from the East Indies.

24

In the green room, Gaüzère has hung impressive nineteenth-century portraits of maharajas and other paintings of the same era. The beautiful cylinder secretary desk on the right is from the Louis XVI period.

25

In front of the majestic Empire-style bed, the focal point is the nineteenth-century maharaja's throne, made in wood and covered in hammered silver. The red and white silk canopy is decorated with a coat of arms. On the left we see a portrait of the master of the house.

26–27

A leopard fur is draped over the back of the sofa in the green room. Through the doorway, flanked by full-length portraits of maharajas, we see the sumptuous decor of the bedroom.

28

A corner of the green room with its classical white marble fireplace and a selection of carefully chosen objects.

31

Walls painted in Tyrrhenian Pink and a black silhouette on an Apple Green medallion: Roberto Bergero is not afraid of bright colors!

32

A forties-style *chauffeuse* has been upholstered in a cherry-colored satin. The canvas rug, painted by hand, is the work of Bergero himself.

33

The living room walls, painted bright pink, form a striking contrast with the Granny Smith Green fire screen and the armchairs covered in a black and white striped fabric.

34–35

In the corner dining room, the tablecloth covering the table is made of a Dedar fabric. Bergero painted the nineteenth-century cane armchair white and chose sunflower-colored silk for the curtains.

36

A Bergero painting, depicting a giant tulip, serves as the head-board for the four-poster bed.

39

An eighteenth-century embossed gilt-bronze lock adorns the entrance to the main floor of the Hôtel de Gesvres.

40

Detail of one of the mask-like heads that ornament the carved stone fireplace in the entrance hall.

41

The imposing entrance hall with its paneling and seventeenth-century fireplace. The gray painted paneling and the black and white flooring reflect the custom of the time of displaying the household's wealth only beyond the entrance.

42

In the Chamber of Mirrors a beautiful seventeenth-century gilded and carved wooden daybed reflects the ostentation of the Louis XIV style.

43

In the duke's room the Louis XV bergères are arranged around a beautiful *lit à la Polonaise* from the end of the eighteenth century.

44

Sèvres porcelain placed on a neoclassical giltwood console.

45

Detail of the Sèvres porcelain figurines.

46

The hanging garden, outside the main floor, gives residents the illusion that their building is surrounded by a romantic park.

49

The dresser created in the seventies by the Disney workshops is called "Hello Kitty." The figurine on the tray is a Japanese manga character.

50–51

The living room has vintage furniture by Marc Newson (b. 1963) and Marc Held (b. 1932). Above the fireplace Yves Gastou has hung a relief sculpture by César Baldaccini (1921–1998) dating from 1960. On the mantelpiece, among the Mickey Mouses created by the French artist André, we discover the rogue *Mickey Viagra*. On the coffee table, is the *Rocking Machine* made famous by the movie *A Clockwork Orange*.

52

In the bathroom the sculpture placed at the corner of the bathtub—a unique work by Alessandro Mendini (b. 1931)—dates from 1985. The chair by Memphis collective's Ettore Sottsass (1917–2007) was designed c. 1979 and manufactured by Alchimia.

53

A series of psychedelic portraits of The Beatles (1967) by Richard Avedon (1923–2004) hangs in the bedroom.

54

An impressive collection of Japanese manga figurines is housed in the guest room.

57

In place of his iconic classical eighteenth-century ceiling decorated with clouds, Garcia selected a midnight blue background for cast aluminum "clouds" made by Hélène de Saint Lager (b. 1957). Equipped with oil lamps, and using a ladder, the "sky" lights up at night!

58–59

In the entry way, Garcia has placed a pair of dressers in carved wood covered with silver leaf, which he created for Baker, the prestigious American furniture manufacturer. The artworks are by Gilles Rimbault (b. 1945). The two stone sculptures are pieces of rock that were found in the Fontainebleau forest.

60–61

In the living room, Garcia has put his signature on the claw-footed bronze stools for Baker, the oversized couch, "constructivist" bookcases, and accordion doors.

62

The designer has always had a penchant for ethnic arts and has managed to incorporate in his new interior a beautiful Ashanti stool, a pre-Columbian statue, and African masks from his collection.

63

Garcia chose a neutral palette for his new home, inspired by the natural colors of wood, rattan, straw, and sand. The cast aluminum table is by Hélène de Saint Lager (b. 1957).

64

The bedroom walls are covered with velvet. On the stairway leading up to the bathroom, Garcia has placed covered terra-cotta pots and *The Four Seasons* by Hubert le Gall (b. 1961), who also created the painting at the top of the steps. Garcia designed the Medusa Lamp for Zonca.

65

Detail of one of the ceramic pots by le Gall.

66

At the entrance a pair of paintings—*Man* and *Woman* by Gilles Rimbault (b. 1945)—hang above the Baker dressers. The sculpture *Insect* is by Hélène de Saint Lager (b. 1957).

69

Behind the eighteenth-century terra-cotta bust of a gentleman, we glimpse part of a painting by Alain Jacquet (1939–2008) entitled *La Vague* (The Wave, 1970).

70–71

The room's beautiful eighteenth-century woodwork was installed by the legendary decorating firm Maison Jansen, who also built the pair of consoles. Hubert le Gall (b. 1961) created a sphere-chandelier adapted to the dimensions of the room, while the chair covered in zebra stripes bears the signature of Marc Held (b. 1932).

72

Apart from the large brass sofa created c. 1970 by an anonymous designer, the living room is full of objects by notable names. The black cabinet is by Jean-Charles Moreux (1889–1956), the *Arrachage* painting is by Jacques Villeglé (b. 1926), the brass and acrylic chair was created by Philippe Hiquily (b. 1925), and the seventeenth-century armoire at the rear of the room is by André-Charles Boulle (1642–1732).

73

For the apartment's master bedroom, Hubert le Gall (b. 1961) has created a true masterpiece: a monumental black and gold lacquered bed and screen.

74

The bathroom walls have been inlaid with mother-of-pearl. The seventies gueridon table is the work of Jacques Duval-Brasseur.

77

View of the first-floor landing. The fluted column is of the Corinthian order.

78

In the small office, also known as the English Room, the walls are hung with cherry-colored gorgoran. The paintings are by Guardi (*Views of Venice*), Hubert Robert (*Porte Saint-Denis* and *Porte Saint-Martin*) and Jean-Baptiste Oudry (*The Pursuits of Louis XV*).

79

The Flemish-born Parisian cabinetmaker Roger Vandercruse—better known as Lacroix (1728–1799)—created the commode (dated 1770) that sits in the Petit Bureau. The terra-cotta medallions are by Jean-Baptiste Nini (1717–1786).

80

The fireplace in the Huet Room, which is named after its famous series of panel paintings by Jean-Baptiste Huet (1745–1811). The scenes, which illustrate the love between a shepherd and a shepherdess, came from an eighteenth-century mansion on rue Laffitte.

81

In the Moïse de Camondo Room, the trim comes from a house on Bordeaux's Cours du Chapeau-Rouge. A painted, carved wooden bed (c. 1765–75) is housed in the alcove. The antique rug is from the Savonnerie carpet factory.

85

In Florence Dostal's dining room a stuffed dog has claimed the mantel for his own!

86

A plump stuffed rooster can be spied through the round hole of the sculptural La Chaise, designed in 1948 by Eames and reproduced by Vitra.

87

In Dostal's office a stuffed Saint Bernard feels perfectly at home among the reproductions of designer furniture by Arne Jacobsen (1902–1971), and Charles (1907–1978) and Ray (1912–1988) Eames.

88

In the kitchen the window is dressed with a generously draped sheer curtain.

89

Dostal takes her meals on a table designed by Ross Lovegrove (b. 1958), beneath a crystal chandelier found in Venice.

90

In Dostal's dressing room, decorated with white curtains and illuminated by crystal chandeliers, a magnificent stuffed elk dominates the space.

91

Pristine white also dominates the bedroom, where the walls are completely draped in muslin. The only contrasting element: a small, embroidered cushion depicting a Jack Russell, Dostal's favorite breed.

92

An aquatic light suffuses the bathroom. Dostal had mosaïc by Pierre Mesguich set into the walls by a craftsman, creating the illusion of a room invaded by branches.

93

Detail of the bathroom wall.

94

Even the lavatory has not escaped the creativity of Dostal, who has glued an impressive number of neon green glass lenses to the walls of her "private retreat."

97

In Didier Rabes' "dacha in the attic," the gallery overlooking the living room is embellished with a carved wooden balustrade that evokes the rustic decor of timber homes in faraway Russia. The eighteenth-century medallion of the profile of Louis XVI comes from the antique dealer Nicole Altero.

98

Rabes has mastered the art of creating the illusion of space. In his "dacha" he managed to maximize the limited square footage by dividing up the area.

99

The "dacha" is the result of the perfect collaboration between an extremely talented designer and a carpenter of matching caliber. Walls covered with wood logs form the perfect backdrop for white linen sofas and red velvet *chauffeuse* chairs.

100

The dining room, with its all-pervading warm tones of blond wood, radiates a cozy and welcoming atmosphere.

101

The kitchen, located in an old attic room, recreates the feel of a rustic idyll.

102

The bathroom, clad in pale wood like the sauna cabins of Nordic countries, is flooded with light.

105

In the generously proportioned entrance hall, the bronze doors and floor inlaid with a white and black marble geometric pattern bear the signature style of Pierre Yovanovitch.

106–107

The cast-iron benches (1919) are by Folke Benson (1886–1971). The bronze chandelier and pair of sconces (c. 1920) are by Paavo Tynell (1890–1973).

108

In the living room, Yovanovitch daringly juxtaposes a pair of chairs by Frank Lloyd Wright (1867–1959), a writing desk by Carl Malmsten (1888–1972), a pair of Ivar Johnson vases, gilt ceramic bowls (1922) by Olof Hult, and sixties andirons. The alabaster ceiling light bears Yovanovitch's own signature.

109

Detail of the living room fireplace with Olof Hult's *Urns of Venus* and a large photograph by Sam Samore (b. 1963).

110

From the living room, you can see the smoking room with its beautiful coral-colored piano designed in 1920 by Gunnar Asplund (1885–1940) and its futuristic chrome ceiling light (1925) by Angvar Almquist.

111

In the bedroom, decorated with exemplary asceticism, the walls are paneled in rosewood. The stool is from the Empire period and the bed designed by Yovanovitch has an alpaca wool cover.

112

The bathroom floor and walls have been completely clad in Galactica marble. The chandelier (1930) is made of Murano glass and the neoclassical gueridon table dates back to the forties.

115

A marble bust of the handsome Apollo Belvedere enjoys pride of place in the niche of the living room.

116

The Louis XVI–style armchairs in the entrance hall are covered with a hand-embroidered fabric created in the workshops of Jean-François Lesage.

117

The walls of the entrance hall were decorated with wide pink and black stripes, executed entirely by hand by the master of the house.

118

Gérard Trémolet loves to mix the most miscellaneous of styles. In the living room he has juxtaposed a Louis XV sofa, a Moroccan coffee table, and a baroque giltwood chandelier.

119

Trémolet loves exotic knickknacks—both contemporary and historical—and did not think twice about placing copies of Chinese porcelain statuettes on rococo-style giltwood consoles that adorn the living room walls.

120

The Oriental-style chairs, on each side of the living room's niche, were created by Elizabeth Garouste (b. 1949) and Mattia Bonetti (b. 1953). Previously, the chairs were used at Le Palace, the premier disco run by the late Fabrice Emaer.

121

Detail of the Le Palace chair and a section of the living room wall where Trémolet has hung a few small paintings.

122

A nineteenth-century plaster bust of Marie Antoinette reigns over the bedroom.

123

Trémolet created the four-poster bed from several existing pieces and dressed it with luxurious silk damask curtains.

124

In his kitchen, Trémolet, a gourmet cook, has gradually gathered a collection of favorite utensils and old copper cookware.

127

The spiral staircase wraps around an oversized column of Murano glass pearls by the French artist Jean-Michel Othoniel (b. 1964).

128–129

In the entrance hall is a giant pearl loop, also created by Othoniel. The artwork on the mantelpiece is by Sophie Calle (b. 1953) and the chair on the left was designed by Paul Mathieu.

130–131

In the living room, Minassian's love of natural materials is evident in the pebble-inlaid fireplace and in the wood-grain patterned silk rugs that he designed. The coffee tables are by Paul Evans.

132

A Xavier Veilhan (b. 1963) mobile floats in the light, lofty space of the living room. The furniture, artwork, and objects include the work of Paul Evans (1931–1987), Colette Guéden (1905–2000), Peter Zimmermann (b. 1956), Guy Limone (b. 1958), Peter Lane, and Pamela Sunday.

133

The ceramic sculpture on the living room coffee table was made by Pamela Sunday.

134

Upstairs, on the dining room wall, Minassian has hung a painting by Bernard Frize (b. 1954). The gondola seats are also by Minassian.

135

A figurative sculpture by Xavier Veilhan (b. 1963) stands at the end of the mezzanine, overlooking the void. This gallery connects the bedrooms and bathroom on the first floor.

136

The kitchen has been renovated in polished steel. The *affichiste* work is by Raymond Hains (1926–2005).

139

In the library, on the mezzanine level, Gavin McKinley set up an unexpected still life featuring boxing gloves and an antique marble head.

140–141

The workshop space transformed by McKinley into a living–dining room. The painting by Glyn Philpot (1884–1937), propped on the easel, is of the painter's favorite niece, the late Gabrielle Cross, immortalized in 1918 at the age of eight.

142

The bookcase occupied a large part of the mezzanine, which also displayed McKinley's beautiful collection of antique frames.

143

In a corner of the living room, McKinley placed a Louis XV *corbeille* (basket-shaped) sofa covered in tan velvet.

144

On the mantelpiece, a drawing by McKinley, an antique head, and a bronze sculpture by Philpot reflect McKinley's penchant for cultural diversity.

145

McKinley boasted of having been among the first collectors of Philpot's work and was particularly proud of having acquired the masterpiece *The Angel of Death*.

146

A bronze Philpot sculpture in the dining room.

149

A plaster shell appliqué by Jean-Charles Moreux (1889–1956).

150

A narrow staircase ascends to the loft. The walls, which imitate classical rusticated stone, are adorned with a series of plaster shell appliqués.

151

The Italian designer Pucci De Rossi (b. 1947) created the chaise longue—a unique piece—in 1982. The portrait of a woman, placed on the floor and leaning against the wall, painted by Eugène Huc (1891–?) in 1927 bears the enigmatic title *Simplicity*!

152–153

The collector has sprinkled his loft with rare, top-quality pieces: *Nu aux fleurs* (Nude with flowers, 1950) by Pierre Molinier (1900–1976), a sofa by Marco de Gueltzl (1958–1992), and paintings and drawings by Jean-Michel Basquiat, Keith Haring, Pierre Alechinsky, and Amédée Ozenfant.

154

In the bedroom a nineteenth-century portrait of a maharaja hangs against a pleated fabric background. The magnificent Empire-style, mahogany, sleigh-bed is Italian.

157

Jean-Jacques Wattel has always been fascinated by the work of twentieth-century ceramic artists. In the large living room a fifties vase by Jacques Innocenti (1926–1958) sits on the "brèche d'Alep" marble mantel.

158

In the large living room the theme is eclecticism. A large, contemporary Aubusson tapestry by Gérard Garouste (b. 1946) is perfectly paired with beautiful Empire furniture, an eighteenth-century statue of Saint Michael, a stool by Elizabeth Garouste (b. 1949) and Mattia Bonetti (b. 1953), and a Savonnerie carpet.

159

The Garouste and Bonetti stool, covered with an Aubusson tapestry that also carries their signature, stands on a "Savonnerie" woven by the Manufacture Saint-Jean.

160

In their bedroom the Wattels prefer to surround themselves with painted white nineteenth-century furniture. The portrait is by Nora Auric (1900–1982), wife of the eminent composer Georges Auric.

161

In the bedroom the fifties white stucco vase fits well with the pale carpet, furniture, and chair by Garouste (b. 1949) and Bonetti (b. 1953).

162

A 1940 stucco panel serves as a background to a porcelain vase from the early nineteenth century.

165

The eighteenth-century mask on the mantelpiece came from the Château de Marly. The jasper and ormolu cup is from the Louis XIV period.

166–167

In the entrance hall, Guy Thodoroff placed a pair of eighteenth-century terra-cotta statues that had previously decorated a gazebo. The Venetian chairs are from the same period and the porphyry goblet is from Russia.

168

The eighteenth-century portrait above the living room fireplace is the work of the Austrian court painter Shey and depicts the Emperor Joseph II, a brother of Marie Antoinette. On the right, a small eighteenth-century armoire is decorated with red lacquer panels, and the designer has hung an anonymous landscape from 1820.

169

This precious lapis lazuli vase with its gilt-bronze mount dates back to the Louis XVI period.

170

A seventeenth-century armoire by André-Charles Boulle (1642–1732) displays an ancient bust and a pair of English candelabra from the English Georgian era. The portrait of a lady is the work of Henri-Pierre Danloux (1753–1809).

171

In one room Thodoroff has placed a bust of Jean Marais by Cocteau and a pair of rock crystal obelisks on top of a sideboard by David Roentgen (1743–1807). The chaise longue was made by Georges Jacob (1739–1814) and the processional cross is Russian.

172

In the green marble bathroom, we find an Empire gueridon table and a crystal bottle by Emilio Terry (1890–1969) from his Château de Rochecotte.

175

Detail of the beautiful wrought ironwork, the work of a friend of Katinka de Montal: designer Joy de Rohan Chabot.

176

By excavating the earth beneath the former orangery, de Montal managed to achieve enough ceiling height to accommodate a mezzanine. The little *chauffeuse* chair is covered with faux ocelot fabric.

177

It wouldn't be Gustavian style without gilt and crystal candlesticks and candelabra. The one on the right was created by the owner.

178

Always inventive and on the lookout for unexpected solutions, de Montal has skirted the table in the entrance hall with a damask fabric bargained for at the Saint-Pierre fabric market in Paris. By dressing the entrance with mirrors, she has created the illusion of depth.

180

In the courtyard, a wall covered with ivy serves as the backdrop for a nineteenth-century neoclassical stone statue, a perfect reproduction of *Terpsichore* by Antonio Canova (1757–1822).

183

In a corner of the room, a nineteenth-century plaster head of the goddess Juno—anonymous—has been placed on a slate table from the forties. The ceramic dove from the fifties was created by the famous Madoura pottery workshop, founded in 1938 in Vallauris, and the Danish School, painting by Andersen dates back to the twenties.

184–185

In the living room, perfect symmetry rules. The medallion armchairs on each side of the fireplace are by André Arbus (1903–1969) and the pair of caramel silk covered chairs was created by Jean-Michel Frank (1895–1941) in the thirties. On the mantelpiece a terra-cotta sculpture by Maurice Saulo (1901–1963) is flanked by fifties fixtures produced by the Charles design house.

186

On a plaster and marble table by Serge Roche (1898–1988), dated 1930, Fourtin has placed a sculpture by Charles Despiau (1874–1946), an early twentieth-century globe, and a bronze sculpture by Ovide Yencesse (1869–1947).

187

At the semicircular end of the dining room, a classic niche houses a marble bust from the Roman period. The brass sheep and sheepskin have been attributed to François-Xavier Lalanne (1927–2008), the star-shaped lamp is a contemporary creation by Tom Dixon (b. 1959), the table is from Jansen, and the terra-cotta head of a woman is the work of the sculptor André Bizette-Lindet (1906–1998).

188

In the bedroom a lovely André Arbus sofa has been placed at the foot of the bed. In front of the window a large, second-century Greek vase catches the daylight that filters in between the purple silk velvet curtains.

191

In the bedroom an eighteenth-century engraving hangs against the lining of a wardrobe from the same period.

192

Guided by the advice of their close friend Jacques Garcia, Alfred van Lelyveld and Olivier Trebosc managed to transform two very ordinary rooms into a true castle hall! The walls are hung with tapestry fragments and the portrait of an ancestor on the left represents van Lelyveld's great-grandfather in Highland dress.

193

The white marble sculpture on the console in the entrance hall is the work of Sarah Bernhardt (1844–1923), who was an accomplished sculptor as well as a famous actress, and depicts her deceased husband.

195

In a corner of the dining room the two antiquarians have installed a beautiful antique *lit à la Polonaise* draped in crimson silk. The ideal place for a postprandial nap.

196

In the bedroom a beautiful toile de Jouy covers the eighteenth-century rustic-style bed and also trims the *lit à la duchesse*.

197

The bathroom is a true "window into the past" thanks to its Directoire bathtub, furniture, and accessories.

198

At the entrance a beautiful white marble eighteenth-century statue stands on a wrapped pedestal from the same period.